Gods' Master Plan for Humanity

Alpha

Trafford rev. 08/04/2011

 www.trafford.com

North America & international
toll-free: 1 888 232 4444 (USA & Canada)
phone: 250 383 6864 ♦ fax: 812 355 4082

About the Author. I was born to Thomas Cannon and Ollie Lee Howard, in Bellville Michigan.

I was the fifth child of eight children born to my parents. My even being born was a act of God.

My mother told me the story, when I was in my forty's , about how I all most didn't get here. She said that when she started having children, she had two boys and two girls. She decided that this was all the children she wanted. Remember back in the late third's when I was born, birth control was unknown to us. So she decided to abort her child. Back then they would use a home remedy to do it. What they would do was take caster oil, and drank the whole bottle, in a attempt to destroy the fetus. She said she thought that she had aborted her baby, me. But she said after nine months, she gave birth to me anyway. Perhaps you are thinking that I might feel unwanted because of it. But I didn't. I believe that I was predestined to enter this world for the sake of the gospel of Christ, for it is the power of God unto salvation. It reminds me of the story of Moses.

Then when he was exposed to perish , the daughter of Pharaoh rescued Him and took him and reared him as her own son.

Acts 7:21(N I V)

In nineteen fifty three I married my late husband R V Thomas. We have six children. (one is deceased) After raising my children, in nineteen eighty seven, The Lord placed in my heart to open a nursing service. I had work in the nursing field for many years. I call it,

CHRISTIAN NURSES FOR CHRIST. I have been reading the book by our Vice Bishop T.D. Jakes. It is call, Reposition yourself. And that is just what I did. We employed over two hundred workers over a six year period. One day my account call me and said, did you know that we had grossed over a hundred thousand dollar that year. I was so busy with the running of the place that I had not noticed what our bottom line look like. I also opened a cleaning service for those that didn't meet the qualification to be a nurse or a nurses aide. TO GOD BE THE GLORY. In the eighty's I opened our first church. After my late husband (Patrick Jennings) died, I closed the church and went to Texas for a while. I also visited LA. For a while. In nineteen ninety four a pastor was leaving his church, and the members ask me if I would consider being there pastor. So after much prayer and counting up the cost, I excepted the position. While pastor of the first church we started, the Lord made me a promise. He said that if I would walk before Him in the beauty of holiness , that He would save my children unto the third and fourth generation. In the month of April I saw my fourth generation. God is not like man that he would lie.

Humbly submitted - Alpha

GOD'S MASTER PLAN FOR HUMANITY

Writer; Ethel Louise Thomas Jennings. Pen Name: ALPHA.

I was inspired to write this book by the Holy Spirit after many years of study and meditation of God's word.

I found that everything has a plan and purpose for every stage of our lives.

Ecclesiastes; 3: 1 To EVERYTHING there is a season and a time for every matter or purpose under heaven. The pattern just keeps repeating it's self day after day year after year century after century. In order to have successful lives we must plug into God's MASTER PLAN FOR HUMANITY.

We can truly say God has a sense of humor, when we look at some of the things He created. For instance the rhinoceros, Who would have thought of putting a horn, of all things in the middle of his face, But when you think about it why not if that's where He decided to put it. Isaiah; 55: 8&9, For my thought are not your thoughts, neither are your ways My ways, says the Lord. For as the heavens are higher then the earth. So are my ways and my thoughts than your thoughts. This is our problem, in our sins we wondered so far from our creator causing a void in our communication, this is the master plan of God to re-connect to man, His prize possession.

I was blessed to have been raised in the country .Have you ever wondered about how God causes the bees to harvest honey. My dad had a strange way of getting the bees, to entice them to stop at our house. First he would find a remote place at the edge of the woods, and then he would build a square box with wooden rods running through it. I am not sure how he knew when the bees were going to fly over our house but he did. He would stand in the yard with a medal spoon and a medal pan. Then he would bang on that pan with that spoon and a strange thing would happen those bees would make a bee line for that bee hive or thy would cover a branch near there and he would open the top of the box and carefully put them inside the box.

I'm not sure how long it took but when he would open the box their were things that look like a filter that you put in the furnace to catch the dust, and it would be filled with honey, the honey would be manufactured in the honey cones. Only God could have devised a plan like that. Heb. 11: 3 By faith we understand that the worlds during the successive ages were framed (fashioned, put in order and equipped for their intended purpose) by the word of God, so that what we see was not made out of things which are visible. Also Romans 8: 2. For the law of the spirit of life (which is) in Christ Jesus (the law of our new being) has freed me from the law of sin and death. God brought us back to Himself. Once again dealing with the spirit of man condemning the works of the flesh. Which brought about the fall in the first place through the lust of the flesh or our appetite. It takes God to help us to control our appetite.

The Importance Of The Mind

Phil: 5 & 6 says, let this same attitude and purpose and (humble) mind be in you which was in Christ Jesus; (Let Him be your example in humility;) Who, although being essentially one with God and in the form of God (possessing the fullness of the attributes which made God), did not think equality with God was a thing to be eagerly grasped or retained, But stripped Himself (of all privileges and rightful dignity). So as to assume the guise of a servant (slave) in that He became like men and was born a human being. Let us take a closer look at that statement, In Genesis 1:26. God said, let us make mankind in our image, after our likeness, and let them have complete authority over the fish of the sea the birds of the air, the (tame) beast and over all the earth and everything that creeps upon the earth. Man is made in the similitude of God. (in his image) we can clearly see the physics of man, but what else did He do that day. I believe man received of the spirit of God that day. Gen. 2:7 Then the Lord God formed man from the dust of the ground and breathed into his nostrils the breath or spirit of life, and man became a living being. This made him a spiritual being. I like to think of it like this, our body is the house the spirit lives in. Why, God is a spirit, all ways was, all ways will be. He is superior in nature and processing His plan made man a replica of Himself, both in dominion and authority . So you know the story, through the lust of the flesh man fall from his God given state. Oh, but look here, came Jesus the second man, Adam coming through the same channel (reproduction system) only God produced him the first man from the dust of the ground, with his seed within himself .Now Jesus even though He wasn't born of the will of the flesh He also had his seed within Himself. John 12:24 says, I assure you, most solemnly I tell you Unless a grain of wheat falls into the earth and dies, it remains (just one grain; it never becomes more but lives) by itself alone .But if it dies, it produces many others and yields a rich harvest-

How Can a Man Be Equal With God

Good question. Because from the beginning equality was in the plan. Let us go back to Geneses 1:28, Then God blessed them and said to them, be fruitful and multiply . Now take a closer look at that statement. Who had just finished re-creating the earth, God. So Adam was given the authority to continue the work He had set up. Man was an extension of God the Father and made in His visible image or the part of God we can see with our visible eye. Man was created to be equal with God the Father in as much as he chose to be. Man was made to live forever in his God given state. I believe when the garden got too small, Adam would have renovated, moving the borders of the garden in to the rest of the earth, but this time with Gods blessings instead of the curse. Remember God had a master plan, the bible says in 1 Peter 1:20 It is true that He was chosen and foreordained (destined and foreknown for it) before the foundation of the world, but He was brought out to public view (made manifest) in these last days(in the end times)for the sake of you.

The Mind Had to Be Re-programmed

In the book of Romans, 12:2 it reads; Do not be conformed to this world but (this age) [Fashioned after and adapted to its external superficial customs], but be transformed (changed) by the [entire] renewal of your mind by its new ideals and its new attitude], so that you may prove [for your selves] what is the good and perfect will of God, even the thing which is good acceptable and perfect [in His sight for you].

The death of Adam's spiritual man, discontinued the previous reason Adam was placed in the garden. From the beginning Adam has a place to start. After Adam had filled the garden with the glory of God and the will of God then he would have continued filling the rest of the earth with the will and the glory of God.

The Earth And Its New Beginning

As you study the bible you will see that something happen between Genesis chapter one and verse one, the place where God had said let their be light was a profound statement, because any one will tell you that darkness empty an with out form is not much of a creation. I believe a catastrophe happened on the earth. In the book of Isaiah chapter fourteen verse twelve says; How have you fallen from heaven Oh! Lucifer son of the morning, how have you have been cut down to the ground .you who weakened and laid low the nations. This tells about Lucifer's great fall and the destruction to the earth and it's inhabitants. also verses sixteen and seventeen; Those who see you will gaze at you and say, Is this the one who made the earth tremble? who shook Kingdoms? Who made the world like a wilderness? and over turned its cities. Who would not permit his prisoners to return home? I am not sure what form of life was here at that time, but I believe that it caused God to give the earth a new beginning.

I believe there was life on earth before Genesis one and verse two. But what form of life, we are not sure. But dinosaur and other evidence of life were found by those that looked at life before our time. Also through the study of rock formation and other ways to measure time the earth appears to be billions of years old. Remember we have a God that is ageless, having no beginning or no end. We can clearly see how the earths former state and the one we see now very. One day I was watching TBN and Benny Hinn was teaching on this very thing I was glade to receive conformation from such a great man of faith.

There Is Nothing New Under The Sun

So many people are still reeling from September eleventh, wondering how such a thing could happen to us here in the good old USA, well it did .I remember clearly that morning watching early morning TV and Brian Gamble was working that morning, he began to report something that was happening at the world trade center their in New York City, I was so devastated by what I saw coming over the net work, it was almost unbelievable, If you had any doubt about, Peter 3:10 But the day of the Lord will come like a thief, and then the heavens will vanish (pass a way) with a thunderous crash, and the {material] ELEMENTS {of the universe} will dissolve with fire, and the earth and the works that are upon it will be burned up. I'm sure you don't any more. I was still in bed when it happened. We were planning our annual recognition banquet, a service where we give certificates to all our workers for that year. We were not going to have it at the hotel that year, we decided to rent a hall so we could do our own cooking, that was the day I was to pay the deposit. The Today show received a news flash, some kind of stray planes was flying into the world trade center. At that time the entire thing was being played out on national television There is more to come, when, where, why, who knows. Only God knows for sure. The word of God reminds us to watch and pray. Also Isa 54:17, reminds the people of God that; no weapon that is formed against you shall prosper, and every tongue that shall rise against you in judgment you shall show to be in the wrong. This {peace, righteousness, security .triumph over opposition} is the heritage of the servant of the Lord {those in whom the ideal Servant of the Lord is reproduced} this is the righteousness or the vindication which they obtain from Me {this is that which I impart to them as their justification} says the Lord.

Survivors Of Nine Eleven

Today I watched the woman that survived ground zero, Loran is her name, how she fought back after being burned over eighty per cent of her body. She lost the use of her hands for a time and the total use of her body while recovering from the fire that all most took her life. Thank God for prayer, determination, good husbands and families. We know that God smiled on her that day, in the mist of all her injury's the thought of her young son and the love of her husband kept her fighting for her life. She was on Oprah's show and you could see that God was with her through it all. Romans 5:5 says ;Such hope never disappoints or deludes or shames us. For God's love has been poured out in our hearts through the holy spirit that has been given to us. While we were yet in weakness (Powerless to help ourselves) at the fitting time Christ died for (on behalf of) the ungodly. As I watched her I was thinking how we put so much stock in how we look on the outside, when our true beauty comes from the inside straight from the heart.

Why Do We Sometimes Choose Darkness

It's amazing how we sometimes refuse the only true light of the world. John; 14:6 Jesus said to him, I am the way and the truth and the life.(or light) When we consider our beginning and the fellowship we had with God our creator, and the authority Adam and Eve had and when you see where they fell, you can see how they strayed from the light. In the light (Christ Jesus) He removed the old transgression, brought us back into fellowship with God the father. He also set up a new kingdom here on earth and drafted us into that new kingdom establishing His righteousness through faith in the earth.

We Must All Experience New Beginnings

I can remember getting married for the first time, So much in love, having found the man of my dreams I thought, we begin planning our lives, well I said, until death do us part, I really meant It, but as you know it takes two to tangle. And life has a way of throwing crave balls at us. We were doomed from the beginning .WELL as they say hind sight is twenty -twenty. First of all neither of us knew what the heck we were doing. I was only sixteen and after the homey moon, if you can call it that, thing begin to go straight down hill. We were out on our own and that fell through. We had to move in with his grand-parents. This took the responsibility off of him and he begin to cheat on the marriage and started a family with someone else. I know some of you know how that feels .After all of that, I was determined to stick it out. If he went out the front door, doing his thing, I WENT out the back door doing my thing, we would wined up at the same dance hall every time. [their was only one dance hall in that small town]. One day I begin to hunger and thirst for the true and living God. My brother who is two years older then I, tried to commit suicide, he had locked himself in this small house where he lived and put a blanket over his head in front of a small gas heater in the front room and turned the gas on. I saw a miracle that day. my sister just happen to come to my house to visit, we decided to go and visit him. you could see his house from where I lived, when we got there his car was in the driveway so we knew he was home. But when we knocked on the door no one answered, the door was locked, but we kept on knocking and all of a sudden the door just opened, there he was not even breathing. I guest my sister drove a hundred miles per hour getting him to the Doctor's office. Now the miracle. Later on I moved into that same house, and it had a dead bolt lock that had to be opened by hand. I believe the Lord sent an angel to open that lock, [with God All Thing Are Possible.} Now God used that incident to bring me under conviction, He said, if that had been you, and you had died, you would have landed in hell. It put an urgency in me for salvation. A Godly fear came over me and I began to search for Him and at the age of nineteen I was born again and He has been the love of my life for over fifty four years.

God's Intention For Man

Let us take a closer look at God's intention for man. God only deals with eternal values in mind. He puts very little values in temporal things, including this life. matt. 16:26 states, what does it profit a man to gain the whole world and forfeit his life [his blessed life in the kingdom of God] or what would a man give in exchange for his [BLESSED LIFE IN THE KINGDOM OF GOD]? I use the word temporal for that is just what it is, for a season, and most cases a very short season. Two paths are set before us at all times, we must choose the God given path that leads to life here, and a better life in the here after.

Job's Experience And God's Intention

In the book of Job God allowed Satan to afflict Job with the lose of his processions and his children, this was a mental affliction at first. Job past that test, his response was, the Lord giveth and the Lord takes away blessed be the name of the Lord, then Satan came back the second time and said to the Lord, Job 2:4-6. Skin for skin, yes, all that a man has will he give for his life. But put Your hand now and touch his bone and his flesh and he will curse and renounce You to Your face. And the Lord said to satan, Behold, he is in your hand; only spare his life. Did you ever wonder why God was so sure that Job would pass the test? well I believe that first of all we will never know what are capabilities are unless we are put to the test. Not only did God know what Job's motives were, He wanted Job to know what his motives were all about. God allowed Satan to test Job, only to find out that Job came out on top both spiritually and naturally, Satan didn't realize that he had been had! First of all we must realize that our lives are in God's hands. Matt. 10:28. And I give them eternal life, and they shall never lose it or perish throughout the age. [To all eternity they shall never by any means be destroyed] And no one is able to snatch them out of my hand. So remember when you are being tested, God knows all about it and He will see you safely through

The Power Of Reconciliation

The meaning of reconciliation is to be bought back into fellowship, and that is what Christ did. Heb, 2:16. For, as we all know, He Christ, did not take hold of angels [the fallen angles, to give them a helping and delivering hand] but He did take hold of the fallen descendants of Abraham [to reach out to them a helping and delivering hand].2Cor;5: 20 say's, So we are Christ's ambassador's,

God making His appeal as it were through us . We [as Christ's personal representatives] beg you for your sake to lay hold of the divine favor [now offered you] and be reconciled to God. Now this placed us back in the game. Also Col. 2:14 Having cancelled and blotted out and wiped away the hand writing of the note (bond) with it's legal decrees and demands which was in force and stood against us (hostile to us). This (note with all it's regulations, decrees, and demands) He set aside and cleared completely out of our way by nailing it to [His] cross.

Two Kingdoms: To Which Kingdom Do You Belong

We that are born again realize what that entails, you have moved from the kingdom of this world, into the kingdom of God's dear son. Col. 1:13.[The Father] has delivered and drawn us to Himself out of the control and the dominion of darkness and has transferred us into the kingdom of the son of love, In whom we have our redemption through His blood,[which means] the forgiveness of our sins. Some Christians are professing Christ but deny the power there of. 2 Timothy 3:5. For [although] they hold a form of piety (true religion),they deny and reject and are strangers to the power of it [their conduct belies the genuineness of there profession] Avoid [all] such people [turn away from them]

Tenant Of The Tunnel

I took this article from (Our Daily Bread) written by Mart De Haan; For 16 years, Kovacs was a tenant of the tunnel."Along with a few others, John lived under ground in an abandoned railroad tunnel in New York City. When Amtrak bought the tunnel and prepared to reopen it, John was forced to live above ground.

According to the New York times, Mr. Kovacs became the first person chosen for a new program designed to transform the homeless into homesteaders," After spending over a third of his life in a railroad tunnel, he left his underground existence to become an organic farmer in upstate New York. He was quoted as saying, The air will be better up there. I'm not going to miss anything .I'm not coming back. If we could see ourselves as our

Lord does, we would realize that every child of God has had a similar experience. We too have been chosen to leave a dark, filthy existence for the dignity of a new life and work. If only we could see our former as clearly as John Kovacs saw his, we too would know that there is nothing worth while in the dark, and no reason to go back. Lord, help us to remember how needy we were when You found us. Forgive us for sometime wanting to go back to the tunnel.

I wandered in the shades of the night

Till Jesus came to me
And with the sunlight of His love
By all my darkness flee.- Van De Vender

Children of the light will not be comfortable in the dark.

How Does The New Kingdom Work?

Thanks for asking, First of all it is governed by the Lord Himself. John 15 6:1 I AM the True Vine, and My Father is the Vine dresser. Any branch in Me that does not bear fruit [that stop bearing] He cuts away trims off , takes away , and He cleanses and repeatedly prunes every branch that continues to bear fruit, to make it bear more and richer and more excellent fruit, you are cleansed and pruned already, because of the word which I have given you [the teachings I have discussed with you]. Dwell in Me, and I will dwell in you .[live in me and I will live in you] Just as no branch can bear fruit of itself without abiding in (being vitally united to) the vine, nether can you bear fruit unless you abide in me. I am the Vine; you are the branches. Who ever lives in Me and I in him bears much fruit(abundant)fruit. However, apart from Me [cut off from vital union with Me] you can do nothing. If a person does not dwell in me, he is thrown out like a [broken -off] branch, and withers ;such branches are gathered up and thrown into the fire, and they are burned.

Sometimes we are so programmed already, how to operate in this system, that we fine it difficult to re-program so we can be successful in the new kingdom. Every road in this life leads to a dead end, the wages of sin is death, But the gift of God is eternal life through (in union with) Jesus Christ our Lord. Rom .6:23 .whatever we obtain in this life, whatever, fame, prestige, wealth, it will come to an end. but eternal life will keep on going and going and going.

Praise God for ETERNAL LIFE. As you grow in Christ, and become connected to His divine will and purpose for your life., Eph.1:18 By having the eyes of your heart flooded with light, so that you can know and understand the hope to which He has called you, and how rich is His glorious inheritance in the saints (His set apart ones),

Being Connected To The Highest Power There Is

Everyone knows that divine power is the highest power there is. Christ Jesus is that power. In Matt. 28: 18 Jesus said; all authority (all power of rule) in heaven and on earth has been given to me. As you grow in Christ your eyes of understanding shall be opened to the divine rudiments of the kingdom of God, which is only given through Christ Jesus, but you must first pull off the old man or the sinful nature that you were born with and except the transformation of Christ through faith. Then and only then will a whole new world open up to you. You will find in your life that you were in bondage , now you are FREE. Now you are free to be what God put you on earth to be, fulfilling your destiny or your purpose in life. John 10:27 says; The sheep that are my own hear and are listening to my voice ; and I know them, and they fellow Me. Also verse 28, says, and I will give them eternal life, and they shell never lose it or perish throughout the ages, {to all eternity they shall never by any means be destroyed.} and no one is able to snatch them out of my hand.

The Best Of Both Worlds

God blessed them and said to them, Be fruitful and multiply, and fill the earth, and subdue it {using all its vast resources in the service of the God and man} and have dominion over the fish of the sea, the birds of the air, and over every living creature that moved upon the earth. I believe when God created the earth, He had Adam in mind. He knew He would need a counter part to take dominion over the earth,

When I was a child I couldn't understand how people knew that I was a child. I was about six at the time and a man came to the door and ask for my father, he ask me why wasn't I in school, I said I don't go to school, as if I had finished school, not thinking about my size. Just plain dumb, now that I think about it. But life would teach me how immature I really was.

My First Remembrance Of Church

I can remember going to church for the first time, they told me this is the house of God, so I got on my toes as not to disturb Him. Reverence must come from the heart of a person.

We find in Hebrews 11:6 Without faith it is impossible to please God. I learned at a early age to talk to Him, and to pray and expect an answer, which takes us back to that age old question, does God hear a sinners prayer? well, let me tell you what I learned, He will respond to His children, wouldn't you?.

My Dad

My dad was a very disturbed man, some would call him a self made man, very insecure in himself, now insecurity will make you afraid of many things. He was insecure in his marriage, causing him to be very cruel to my mother, and us kids, and as the older kids reach there teens he began to fear retaliation from them, and it made him even meaner. I can remember him taking my eldest brother to the barn and beating him until his eyes swollen   shut, there were four children older then myself, they began to plot to kill him, but my mother would say to them, that's your father, don't you touch him.

As 1 write this book, I am please to report that we just celebrated her one hundredth birthday in two thousand four, he passed away in nineteen ninety eight at the age of 96.

My Mom

She was born in York Alabama, and raised in the south, my dad also was raise in the south. They met and were married. My dad had a brother who lived in Ecorse, Michigan, and they moved in with him. He was hired at Ford motor company, and retired from their after forty year of employment. They started a family. To this union eight children were born. My mother is a very loving person, I often say I will never be the woman she is. After a few years, they moved to the country where we started to farm, there were very few conveniences , my dad worked and we had to do the farming.

This was during the depression and things were very hard. We had electricity but no refrigerator. An ice man, we called him, would come to our house three times a week, pulling a wagon with a horse. We did have inside plumbing. the house was heated by a pot belly stove that sat by a chimney in the kitchen. Both came through the guise of slavery . When we would visit our grand parents in the south it look down right primitive, the house sat on four bricks and you could lay in bed and count the stars.

Getting back to our farm in Michigan, their were all kinds of farm animals that had to be attended to, and their was the garden, and fields and fields of corn, my mother worked hours upon hours in the fields, milking cows ,feeding chickens and after all that, caring for a husband and eight children, it sound like slavery to me. She also endured mental and physical abuse.

She Tried To Drown Her Pain

My mother became an alcoholic, I can remember when she didn't drank anything stronger then Kool-aid. To top that, he began to make bootleg liquor in our kitchen. My mother started drinking. I have found when you try to drown your troubles with alcohol, drugs, smoking or what ever your vice might be, it only makes it worse, because when you started you only had one problem, but now you have several more problems. The only way you can handle life's problems is to face them. It is very hard for a mother to watch her children be abused. We put the 'dys' in dysfunctional family. The abuse would get so bad that she would leave the family for weeks at a time, but she would always come back because of us kids, but one day she didn't come back, I'll tell you about that later. The fighting was the hardest to endure, I would be awakened in the middle of the night, by her, screaming for her life. He would beat her in the head and blood would be every where. In the morning she would have a big smile on her face so we wouldn't be worried. The remembrance of these things brings me to tears as I write.

A Tragedy Hits

I was born during the depressing of the thirties, during that time meat was quarantined and you couldn't buy or sell it. One of the things my dad did was raise hogs and he would take them to the market and sell them, but because of the quarantine he couldn't do that, well he started a sale of black market meat. He would put the meat under the bed of the truck. At that time he was hauling left over bread from peter pan bakery, in Detroit MI. he would feed the old bread to the hogs, so he would put the meat under the bed of the truck and the old bread on top of the bed . He was stop many times but when the police would look, they would only see the old bread. Now he had dreams about building a new home, and after a few years he had saved enough money to do just that. He bought a peace of land about five miles from where we lived. He and my brothers and any help he could get started to build. I can remember him being preoccupied with this new project, and the fighting and auguring stopped. When the house was completed and we were preparing to move in, my dad came home one morning with tears in his eyes. He worked after noon's and on his way home he discovered that some one had burned our new home to the ground. That was a sad day at our house, you can image how we felt.

Now you would have to had known my dad to understand what he did next. He had spent all his savings, and back then very few black men could qualify for a loan and the nation was in a depression, or just starting to recover from one. Also he had lost money when the banks closed .

Plan B

Things really got tight around our house ,as he began to re-build our house in that same spot. The next house was just a shadow of what the other home was. He put our old house and the land he owned up for sale. I can remember the day we moved into that house, he was forced to use rejected material and it looked it.

Barefoot And Pregnant

This was one of my dad's strategies to keep my mother bare foot and pregnant. She had very little education and had to do manual labor when she was in the work a day world. My baby sister was born in 1946, we moved in our new house in 1948, she was two years old. One of the things that keep my mother around so long was her children. She said many times, that was the only thing that keep her there.

The War Began Again

The fighting and the abuse caused the older children to began to leave much earlier then they should have. My older brother had already left before we moved, my sister was the next oldest, she become his next target to drive her away. When he would jump on my mother, she would jump in the fight, as Dr. Phil would say, there would be two dogs in the fight against one. She to ran away, she was the first person in our family to become born again.

She moved to Muskegon MI. and their she met the man of her dreams, and they got married and started a family.

A Safe Place To Hide

My mother had a sister who lived in Muskegon MI. When my mother got to the place she couldn't take any more fussing and fighting, she would go to aunt Dee's, who lived in Muskegon. So when my oldest sister left home this was a safe place to hide. Aunt Dee was a trip, as they say. Her behavior reminded me of a adult who never really grew up. She and uncle Marvin, her common law husband, would start partying on Friday nights and would continue way into the following week, for poor people they sure did waste a lot of food, if someone was in the kitchen cooking and it didn't look right they would throw the hold thing away. Well in our house that just didn't happen, with ten mouths to feed, you got it right the first time!.

The Straw That Broke The Camel's Back

My mother told us that the only thing that kept her there was her kid's. My dad worked the after noon shift and sometimes he would get off early, and he would sneak up on us just to see what we were doing, their were always lots of thing to do on a farm, before he would leave for work he would lay out this long list of things to be done by the next day, but the minute his car got out of sight we would drop everything and we would play until our heart's were continent. Now I need to tell you that wasn't such a bad idea. I believe kid's today have to much time on there hands, if they are given more constructive things to do they would n't be out there shooting up schools and doing crazy stuff like that. As I was saying he would sneak back just to see what we were doing. One day he came back home early, my mother had stepped out to visited some neighbors and while she was gone he came back home, and he was standing in the front door, now their were three steps to climb to enter the door, when she started to come up the steps he took his foot and kicked her in her face, she told us later that a voice told her to leave and not to come back and if she did he would take her life, she was obedient and she never returned to the house to live again. This was the straw that broke the camel's back.

Take A Licking And Keep On Ticking

I know some of you remember that saying from the Timex commercial, well that's just what I learn to do. I was being groomed for life's struggles. This book is titled GOD'S MASTER PLAN FOR HUMANITY. I am attempting to portray how our lives are preordained by God even before conception. This is why it is so important to be born again. St John 3:3 Jesus answered him, I assure you, most solemnly I tell you, that unless a person is born again (anew, from above), he cannot ever see (know, be acquainted with, and experience) the kingdom of God. All of us got here through birth, so that is not a new thing to us. Even though we were to young to remember it. But when you are born again you should have full knowledge of that process because when the tempter (the devil) comes after you again you can remind him of the new birth that has been recorded in heaven on your behalf. Galatians 6: 15 For neither is circumcision (now) of any importance, nor uncircumcision, but (only)a new creation (the result of a new birth and a new nature in Christ Jesus, the messiah). It reminds me of a marriage ceremony, even though physically you are the same, spiritually things have changed. NOW to those of you that didn't know it, marriage is ordained by God. Here in the twenty first century, I see so much about marriage, no wonder over fifty per cent of the marriages end up in divorce. Remember marriage is made in heaven, it is a binding agreement made before God.

When I became born again, I was a real basket case, I need to tell you that their is no case to hard for God. Phil. 1:6 And I am convinced and sure of this very thing, that He that begin a good work in you will continue until the day of our Lord Jesus Christ [right up to the time of His return] redevelop [that good work] and perfecting and bringing it to full completion in you. I didn't know it, but that perfecting work had begun in me. When you are a child you don't understand life's lessons, but when you grow up, then you can understand ,look back and understand life's lessons.

Some Terms They Had Down To A Science

There are certain cultures that developed their own style of certain use of certain words, for instance, you know the reference to the moving of one's bowel's, they (my mom and dad) had that word down to a science, they would say SHI1IT, back and forward to one another in concert style, now that I look back on it, it was hilarious. I cant remember very many good times when I was growing up. my dad loved Christmas, they were big on the Santa Clause bit, they were so convincing that I was sure that there was a Santa clause. You know I have mixed feelings about the practice of telling your children this myth, when you tell them fairy tales like snow white and the seven dwarfs, it teaches them to dream, so even though I chose not to continue the practice, 1 can't see the harm, well I can hear you thinking, it is a myth or a un-truth, but I still believe it causes them to dream.

Well This Looks Like The End

You know I told you that my mother just celebrated her one hundredth birthday last year. Well I got a call this week, it was my sister (my mother lives with her) she said mother was very weak and not eating or drinking water as she should. She will be one hundred and one next month, I'm praying that she'll make it. We must have a positive out look about life and death. Just as it takes faith to live by, it also takes it to die by. Heb. 11:6 say's, Without faith it is impossible to please God, for he that cometh to God must first believe that He is and He is a re- warder of those who diligently seek Him out. This kind of faith is good to live by and also to die by. We just returned home from magi-feast this week, the theme was Focus On The Family. Bishop T. D Jakes started the conference off with the story about Jacob, when he was about to die, called his twelve son's around his bed . Now it took faith to believe that his predictions would come to past. this is called dyeing faith or faith to die by. Ref. Gens.49:1

Update

On February 7 my mother died. We called her Ma Dear, oh what a legacy she left for her heirs, eight children (three are deceased) 36 grandchildren, 97 great-grandchildren, 90 great-great-grandchildren and a host of nieces, nephews, cousins, and friends. About five hundred persons attended her funeral. We are experiencing what I call the changing of the guards, I noticed while at the funeral that the ushers would relieve each other ever so often, two of them would be standing by the casket and on Q two more of them would come and stand in front of them and the two that were standing guard would move and the others would take there place, I called it the changing of the guards. This is who we are in my age bracket, we are experiencing, our generation, and its giving away to the next generation ,and it is God's Master Plan.

What Are We Going To Do With Those Twins

On August 29th 2005 we experienced one of the most devastating hurricanes in the history of our country. Katrina, and Rita followed close behind her. This region has not been the same nor can it ever be. We were blessed, even though we live in the Mobile Alabama area, we are twenty miles north of it, in a small town call Chunchula, Alabama. I will never forget that terrible day that Katrina hit our area. Every news bulletin was watching the progression of the hurricane as it twist and turned making it's way to the gulf of Mexico. We moved down here from Toledo, Ohio in June of 2004. In 1996 at the age 94, my dad realized that he wasn't going to be able to live alone any longer. After he and my mother divorced he remarried at the age of seventy two. One of the neighbors in the town where my dad lived, started kicking it. Her husband had died. A few years later, she and my dad got married. If there ever was a saint of God, she was one. We called her Hay. My dad was a master manipulator, he knew how to turn on the charm. He was good at saving his money, and he drove a big Cadillac, anyway, they got married. Hay had children by her first husband. And they knew how cruel he was to our mother. And they told him in no uncertain terms if he ever laid a hand on their mother, that they were going to kill him. Well, it worked, as far as we know, he never did. But you must know by now that mental cruelty is just as bad as physical cruelty. I often say that their generation was made of a different stock then we were. Just think about it, would we have been able to endure the cruelty of slavery the way they did, I don't think so. He would n't allow her children to come to their house to visit her. And I'm being nice out of respect for my dad. When Hay died, it left him all along . Then he found out that he had stage four prostate cancer. Now it was a brand new ball game. His options were either go to a nursing home, or eat crow, and ask one of us kids for help. At that time their were only five of us left, my brother had been helping him out for a while. For some reason he started coming to Ohio where I live, and staying with me and my family. Before he died. He turn his estate over to me. And that is how I got to Alabama. I started a church in Toledo, Ohio in nineteen eighty three. We called it Christ Garden of Prayer. As I moved closer to retirement, I made the decision to relocate to Alabama. I turned the church over to my oldest son, Troy J. Thomas and I became their overseer.

Part Two

We are entering the last few days of summer, and we can truly say we are blessed. In all my days on this earth I have never seen a time like we are living in today. First of all the weather is doing it's own thing. The Bible talked about in the last days strange things would happen in the elements. Earthquakes in strange places. Also wars and talk of wars everywhere. It is making the true believers look up for our redemption is very near.

Everything is changing, at your house my house and the white as we have know it. But we know that there is a foundation that we can stand on, and it is sure, that is the word of God. This is the only road map that will lead us to our rightful destiny. There was a time in my life when I new that the party was over. After I got married and started a family, I realized that my children were the most important thing in my life. I deal with a lot of inter city young people, they are influenced very easily, so many are being raised with out fathers in the home. Even at that it can be done, with Gods help.

Some of the things that causes them to go astray are bad influences. There teen years are very challenging, they want to be accepted by their peers. If they could get through those times, they would fine that everything will be just fine. They will learn to think for themselves. I was blessed to have raised six children, there father left our home when they were very young. Now I am enjoying my third generation. And I am very sure that before I leave this earth, the fourth generation will arrive. Low self-esteem is one of the things that holds many of our young people back. I raised one of my granddaughters, brought her from the hospital to my house. When she started to date she would make bad choices. So when she finished high school I ask her why she made the choices she did, she said that some of the boys she liked didn't seem to like her. From my experiences some guys are not attracted to certain girls because of the way they carry themselves, if they are looking for a loose girl, they will not choose a good one because that is not what they want. I am advising our young people to not take the first thing that comes along. There is no hurry, take there time and see if they are compatible to your standards, your faith, also just the way you believe life should be lived. 2co. 6:14, Speaks about not being unequally yoked with sinners and unbelievers. After all, marriage was ordained by God, and to live out side of his blessings will make a unhappy home.

The Process of Salvation

St. Luke 19:10 reads, The Son of Man came to seek and to save that which was lost. Also Luke 4:4 reads, Man shall not live by bread alone, but by every word that comes from the mouth of God. Isa. 54:13 And all my (spiritual children shall be disciples (taught by the Lord and obedient to His will). And great shall be the peace and undisturbed composure of your children. John 6:44. No one is able to come to me unless the Father draws him and gives him the desire to come to me, and [then] I will raise him up [from the dead] at the last day. Verse 45, And they shall all be taught of God [have Him in person for their teacher] Everyone who has listened to and learned from the Father come to Me. Verse 47: I assure you , most solemnly I tell you , he who believes in Me [who adheres to, trusts in, relies on, and have faith in Me] has (now possesses) eternal life.

Do Your Part

We must do our part, faith comes by hearing and hearing of the word of God. This I know for sure everyone that looks for Him will find Him. Time and chance will come to us all. Seek and you will find, knock and He will open unto you. I was so impressed by the election of our first African-American President. When I was a little girl being raised under the shadow of slavery, Even though we were raised in the north our parents were from the south. Have you every hear the saying that you can take a person out of the south but you can't take the south out of that person. Well I found that to be true. My mother had a little saying she would say from time to time, she said there is coming a time when the bottom rail will become the top rail. I had no idea what she meant then, but now I understand.

How We Got Here In the First Place

I watched the movie Roots many times, and I believe that it was Gods master plan for the African American people to get here in the first place. Now we see His ability to turn things around. Sometimes we fail to realize, or to understand who God really is. 1cor. 10:26, says; The earth is the Lords and everything in it is His also.

If you are to be successful at what you do and still have peace with God, you must follow the plan He has for your life. Step one, you must have faith in God. Rom: 11:36. Reads: From Him and through Him and to Him are all things. [for all things originated with Him and came from Him; all things live through Him, and all things center in and tend to consummate and to end in Him.] to Him be glory forever! Amen(so be it) I preached a sermon at our church entitled, Only You can roll away the stone. In the book of Mark; 16:3. And they said to one another, Who will roll away the stone for us out of the door of the tomb?. I am saying to you that only You can roll away the stone that death has placed at the door of your heart.

And that can only be done through faith in Jesus Christ. Matt; 11:28&29 is an invitation to all that will receive Him. Come to me, all you who labor and are heavy-laden and overburdened, and I will give you rest.[I will ease and relieve and refresh your souls] Take My yoke upon you and learn of me, for I am gentle (meek) and humble (lowly) in heart, and you will find rest for your souls. This is the way we should respond to His message of truth.

It's All About Attitude

I had the opportunity to speak at our national convention last year. I was ask to speak on I kings 19: 1-3. Why the let down after victory. It talked about when Elijah had called fire from heaven and consumed burnt sacrifice on the alter he had made. But when Jezebel said she would take his life for it, he became afraid and ran for his life, and went through a depression for it. Fear will cancel your faith quickly. I defined the word fear like this. Facing the Enemy with Artificial Reasoning. There is no place for fear in faith. IF YOU provide the faith God will provide the miracle. He can take you through the fire.

Shadrach, Meshack, and Abednego

One of my favorite stories in the bible is the one about the three Hebrew boys. I pray that you believe what you read in the bible, for you see that which is impossible for man to do, is possible for God to do. (ref.)Dan.3:25. He answered, Behold, I see four men loose, walking in the mist of the fire, and they are not hurt! And the form of the fourth is like a son of the gods! Phil; 5:8 reads, let this attitude and purpose and [humble] mind be in you which was also in Christ Jesus : [let Him be your example in humility:] Who although being essentially one with God and in the form of God [possessing the fullness of the attributes which made God, God]. did not think this equality with God was a thing to be eagerly grasped or retained, But stripped Himself [of all privileges and rightful dignity].so as to assume the guise of a servant (slave) . In that He became like man and was born a human being. And after He had appeared in human form, He abased and humbled Himself [still further] and carried His obedience to the extreme of death even the death of the cross!. So if you change your attitude you can change your life.

Perception

If you change the way you look at things, you can change your life. This is why the education system works, it causes you to add to the way you look at things. It is call knowledge. And if you keep on adding to your knowledge you will become wise. NOTHING can make you any wiser then the man that wrote the book on wisdom, and that is God. He is the author and finisher of our faith. Genesis one reads, In the beginning GOD. He is the only one that can say He always was and is, and always will be. When you except His Son (Jesus) as your personal savior and allow Him to come into your life through His spirit, then your spiritual eyes will become opened and you will begin to experience a greater life then you have ever known. St. John 15:26. Reads. But when the helper comes, whom I shall send to you from the Father, the Spirit of truth who proceeds from the Father, He will testify of Me. PLEASE don't stop until you have had this experience.

The Signs Of The Times

One of the things that you must learn is the road signs when you are taking the test for your drivers licence, well the kingdom of God has signs also. Matt. 24:3, reads like this. While He was seated on the mount of Olive, the disciples came to Him privately and said, tell us, when will this take place, and what will be the signs of your coming and of the end(the completion, the consummation of the age?(4), Jesus answered them, Be careful that no one mislead you [deceive you and lead you into error.(5), For many will come in (on the strength of) my name [appropriating the name which belongs to Me] , saying I am the Christ(the Messiah) and they will lead many astray.(13),But he who endures to the end will be saved. (14),And this good news of the Kingdom (the Gospel) will be preached throughout the whole world as a testimony to all nations and then will the end come.

Times & Seasons

In the book of Eccl.3:Reads: To Every Thing there is a season, and a time for every matter or purpose under heaven:(2), A time to be born and a time to die, a time to plant and a time to pluck up what is planted. Heb;9:27; reads, And just as it is appointed for (all)men once to die, and after that the (certain) judgment,(28),Even so it is that Christ, having been offered to take upon Himself and bear as a burden the sins of many once and for all. Will appear a second time, not to carry any burden of sin nor to deal with sin, but bring to full salvation those who are [eagerly constantly, and patiently] waiting for and expecting Him.(A man). So we know that the time for His second coming (Christ) is rapidly approaching. (A man). So we must be a ware of Gods timing and His seasons. We that are born again must be careful not to allow the cares of this life, to blind us from the time and season for His soon return.

We are living in a time when we are expecting for things to get back to what I call business as usual, or status quo, but I have some news for you, that ain't going to happen. Read; Luke 21:34, But take heed to yourselves and be on guard, lest your hearts be overburdened and depressed (weighted down) with giddiness and headache and nausea of self-indulgence, drunkenness, and worldly worries and cares pertaining to(the business of) this life, and (lest) that day come upon you suddenly like a trap or noose; (35), For it will come upon all who live upon the face of the entire earth. If any one knows what the future holds for this world, God does. HE (GOD) started it, and He is going to end it. Read; Rev; 1:7&8, Behold, He is coming with the clouds , and every eye will see Him, even those who pierced Him, and all the tribes of the earth shall gaze upon Him and beat their breast and mourn and lament over Him. Even so [must it be] Amen (so be it).

I was looking out of my bedroom window this morning it was about eight thirty, and I saw city trucks pulling up across the street from my house. We have been experiencing an invasion of ash bore worms in the trees on our street. The city is starting to remove them. These tree have been there for over thirty years, they have grown very big and tall. I am reminded of something Jesus said in Matt;15:12-13. Then the disciples come and said to Him, Do you know that the pharisees were displeased and offended and indignant when they heard this saying? (13), He answered , Every plant which My Heavenly Father has not planted will be torn up by the roots. The system as we know it will be replaced, I believe very soon. Matt. 25:13. Reads, Watch therefore [give strict attention to and be cautious and active], for you know neither the day nor the hour when the Son of Man will come .All signs are pointing to His soon return, it is time for us to get ready and stay ready.

The Under Cover Boss

There is a new program on TV, it is called, The under cover boss. I would like to equate this show with insight I got from the word of God. St. John 1:1, reads; In the beginning [before all time] was the Word (Christ), and the word was with God , and the word was God Himself. (Ref) [Isa.9:6]reads, for to us a child is born ,to us a Son is given; and the government shall be on His shoulders, and His name shall be called wonderful Counselor, Mighty God, everlasting Father [of Eternity] Prince of Peace. (John) v;(2) reads; He was present (Christ or the Word) originally with God. (V,3;) reads, All things was made and came into existence through ;(Christ or the Word) and without Him was not even one thing made that has come into being.(v,4) reads, In Him was life ,and the life was the light of men.(Christ).Now in the TV show this CEO of a certain company disguises himself, changes his name and becomes a trainee of the company he owns. He takes on the task of a ordinary laborer, experiencing first hand the work a day world of his employees. That is exactly what God did for us. Since God is a spiritual being and He can not be seen by the natural eye, so He disguised Himself in the form of a man and walked among us in a body that we could see and touch, and experience His presences and be touched and taught by Him. St. John; 1:10. Reads; He came into the world, all though the world was made through Him ,the world did not recognize Him[did not know Him] v,(11); He came to that which belong to Him [to His own –His domain, creation, things, world] and they who were His own [the jews] did not receive Him and did not welcome Him. V,(12); But, to as many as did receive and welcome Him , He gave the authority (power, privilege, right) to become the children of God, that is to those who believe in (adhere to trust in , and rely on) His name. Now the TV program, the under cover boss, in the end, he revels who he really is and he evaluates the things he has observed, and make improvements on the shortcomings of the company and also in many cases, ease the heart-ships that are sometimes caused by lack of insight. He also awards assistance to his loyal workers. Many times by giving them raises, sending them on vacations and many more things, that give them incentive to work even harder to make that Co. Continue to succeed in this very competitive system. That is exactly what our God did though Jesus our Lord, Col;2:9. Reads, For in Him the whole fullness of the deity (the Godhead) continues to dwell in bodily form[giving complete expression of the divine nature]. Jesus our Divine mediator between man and God. As the saying go, He paid the cost to be the Boss. Oh, I can hear the siren's going off in your head, how can I plug into this divine system. I am so glad you ask. First, you must have faith in the word of God, it is called believing, then you must put your faith into action by repenting of your sins, fine a place right NOW and ask God to forgive you, and you must know and believe that He did. Now you have to feed your faith. This step is very important, ask God to lead you to a place of fellowship, not just any place but a bible believing, bible teaching church.

How The Lord Found Me

Earlier on I told you how my brother try to commit suicide , and the Holy spirit spoke to me and said, Ethel, if that had been you and you had died you would have went straight to Hell. Believe me if you ever hear the voice of the Lord you will know that it is HIM. Well, that encounter with the Lord put an urgency in my quest for the true and living God. I would not settle for anything less. I begin to hunger and thirst for Him. Going back to my roots, visiting the church that I grow up in but that did not satisfy me. The answer was right in view of my house. The year was nineteen fifty seven. A small church was being build on my street. The spirit of the Lord spoke to me and said, I want you to visit that church today. Guess what day it was, yes you guessed it, it was Sunday. I will never forget that day. When I stepped into that building there was a pot-belled stove that they were using for heat in the winter months. It was very quaint and unfinished, but to me I was stepping into the presence of royalty. I can't remember a word the pastor said, but when the alter call was extended , it was like a force was leading me to go to the alter that day. All I knew was this was my day to receive the Lord and He pardon my sins and filled me with His Holy Spirit. My life has never been the same. (PRAISE GOD FOR HIS UNSPEAKABLE GIFT).

Gods Unspeakable Gift

I would like to enlighten you concerning Gods unspeakable gift. There are something's we experience in life that has a moving effect on our lives, but there are something's that has a PROFOUND effect on our lives. The best way that I can explain it is, that you will experience a change or a transformation in your life. You will have a totally new leash on life, your inter most being will come alive with a remarkable in sight that you have never experience before. (Read) St. John 3:1-36. If I may, I would like to highlight some of the teaching of Jesus. Nicodemus was a pharisees who heard about the uniqueness of Jesus, so he decided to pay Him a visit. But he went by night so know one would know. A pharisee was a group of men made up of an ancient Jewish group that observed both the written and the oral law. They were classed as mister know it all's But Nicodemus just could not figure this man called Jesus out. So he went to check Him out. Let's see what he found out. He started out by telling Jesus, as(Oprah) says in her magazine, what he knew for sure. (V)2, He begin by saying, Rabbi (teacher) We know and are certain that You came from God, for no one can do these signs (these wonderful works, these miracles-and produce the proofs) that you do unless God is with him.(v)3. Jesus answered him, I assure you, or(this I know for sure) that unless a person is born again (a new from above), he cannot even see (know, be acquainted with, and experience) the Kingdom of God. (4) then Nicodemus ask how does that work, can a man enter the second time into his mothers womb and be born again when he is old? (V)5. Jesus said, I kid you not, unless a man be born of water and spirit, he can not even enter the Kingdom of God.(ref) Ezek.36:25&26. They were promised a new heart and a new spirit, also He would remove there stony heart and give them a heart of flesh (a tender) heart v.(7). you must believe me, every one that come to me for help, must be born again from above. V.(15), talks about eternal life is a choice, either you chose eternal life or eternal damnation v.(16) is one of the most quoted verses in the bible, that, God so loved the world that He gave His only begotten Son, that who so ever believe in Him should not parish but have everlasting life. or(live forever) someday. V.(17),Jesus told Nicodemus that He was not here to judge the world (this time) but His mission was to bring salvation or to (offer hope) to a hopeless world. But you must remember that it is up to YOU to make that choice. It is like this, whosoever will, be persuade by there own mind will be excepted. But there will come a time when we will be judged. V. (18).reads.----but he that does not believe in Him is already convicted and has already received his sentence, because he or she has not believed in and trusted in the name of the only begotten Son of God.(He is condemned for refusing to let their trust rest in Christ's name.)We were ALL born on God's death row, because of our sinful nature that our fore fathers left to us. Or we inherit it from Adam & Eve. And that's the way it is.(ref.)Roms3:23.reads, Since all have sinned and are falling short of the honor and glory which God bestows and receives v.(24),reads, [all] are justified and made upright and in right standing with God. Freely and gratuitously by His grace through the redemption which is [provided]in Christ Jesus. So that's the way it is.

Love Love Love

Have you ever felt unloved, you are not alone. I remember after I was born again for a while, things begin to go bad in my marriage. I never stopped praying for my husband after I was saved. I was being told that the sanctified mate would sanctify the other mate, but I found out that salvation is a personal decision between that person and God.1Cor.7: 15,states,But if the unbelieving partner [actually] leaves ,let them do so; in such [a cases the remaining] brother or sister is not morally bound. But God has called us to peace. But I would not give up, I just kept on believing that he would receive the lord as his personal savior and then we would be one happy family in Christ. NOT. It just did not happen. So I went back to the Lord in prayer, asking why was it not happening, and this is what he said, Ethel every one will not except the plan of salvation it is an individual choice. No one can make that decision for you, only you can except GODS MASTER PLAN for your life. I will never forget that day when I was doing the dishes, I was feeling so forsaken and un-loved. And out of nowhere came this voice in my mind, and this is what He said. Greater love have no man then this, that one would lay down his life for a friend. St.John;16:13. Now a day this generation is doing some stinking thinking. They would have you think that having sex is love. I beg to differ. First of all sex was created by God for the sole reason of procreation, and it was only to before a man and his wife. It was only to be confined to one man and one woman. Sex was to be an expression of ones love for another. MALE AND FEMALE. This is God's master plan.

Some Things Can Not Be Changed

There are some things that cannot be changed. This I know for sure, the word of God can not be changed. Ps. 119:89 Says, Forever O Lord your word is settled in the heavens. Now when you understand the way God does things, then you can understand His master plan. He (God) stood in the beginning and declared the ending. Even though He followed His plan from the beginning He knew where the turns were. We travel a lot, and in order to get to where we are going there are many turns, but in order to get where we are going, these turns are needed, but if we follow the road map, we will reach our destination. And our destination should be life and peace in this life, and eternal life after this life. That is Gods master plan for human beings on this earth. But the decision is up to you. You may choose life or death. If you could ask your friends that have gone on before you, I wonder what they would have to say about the choices you are making for yourself. In the book of Luke, chapter 16: 19-31. It told a story about a very rich man who clothed himself in very rich things, and ate very good food every day. And at his gate was dropped off a bigger named Lazarus. His body was covered with sores. He would have been satisfy with the crumbs that fell from the rich mans table. But the dogs had more compassion then the rich man. Now they both died. Lazarus was carried by the angles and placed in the bosom of Abraham. [the father of faith] but the rich man was in a place of torment. When his eyes were opened he saw Lazarus resting in the bosom of Abraham. Then he cried out, Father Abraham, please have mercy on me and send Lazarus just to dip his finger in some water and cool my tongue, for I am in anguish in this flame. But Abraham had some bad news for him. He said, child, remember that in your lifetime fully received comforts and delights, and Lazarus in like manner discomforts and distresses ; but now he is comforted here and you are in anguish. Note, Please don't look to get any compassion in hell, for that is just to late. The rich man was asking a favor of Abraham, now listen to this, he is asking Father Abraham to sent Lazarus to his fathers house and worn his five brothers not to make the same mistake he did. " Daa." He should have thought about that when something could have been done about it. Trust me when I say prays sent from Hell will not be answered. Today is the time to repent of your sins.[to get ride of that curse of sin that was past down from our fore fathers and receive forgiveness through the blood of our Lord and savior Jesus Christ. You don't have to wait until you get to church, do it now. Then believe by faith that God has forgiven you of your sins. Now the next step is very important. You must find a good Bible believing church, there are things you must do to continue to grow in your faith. Just as I had to learn to trust God through his word, you will also learn how to be a child of the King and that is Christ Jesus. There is a song that I learned in vacation bible school. Out of all the things I can remember as a child, this is one thing that stuck in my mind when I was looking for peace with God. I can remember being pick up for vacation bible school. The church was near our house. This is the song. The title is trust and obey. It went like this. Trust and obey, for there is no other way, to be happy in Jesus, but to trust and obey. You will never know how many time that song has came to my rescue when I felt that I had nowhere to turn.

We Are A New Creation

Thank God for new beginnings. I would experience a new beginning every time I would have a new baby. You that are mothers know that after the nine months of waiting for the baby to come, and for me for those last few weeks I couldn't sleep. Somebody said if a man had to have a baby, that their wouldn't be any children at all. Anyway, after it was over and I would hold my new born baby in my arms, it was like a new beginning for me. Life is what you make of it, and with Gods help you can make it whatever YOU want it to be. One thing I find in being born again is that there is a refreshing that comes over your life. It's like moving out of an old house and into a new one, everything is fresh and new. Another thing that I like about being born again is that the pass is just that, the pass. 1John 3:1, reads. See what [an incredible] quality of love the Father has given (shown , bestowed on) us , that we should [be permitted to] be named and called and counted the children of God! And so we are! The reason that the world does not know (recognize, acknowledge) us is that it does not know (recognize, acknowledge) Him. You that are truly born again, enjoy your new life in Jesus, after all He payed the price that you could. I am not boasting when I say with Gods help it has been fifty four years that I repented of my sins and excepted Jesus Christ as my Lord and savior. I can truly say that everyday with Jesus is sweeter than the day before. I'm awaiting His soon return. As you look around , you can see that things can't get much more critical than they are now, but there is hope for this world and that hope is Christ Jesus. There is a song we sing, it go's like this. On Christ the solid rock I stand, all other ground is sinking sand. That is a true song, the only sure place for us to stand is in the word of God. This I know for sure that in the end Gods word will be the only thing left standing. In the book of Rev.20:12. Reads, I [also] saw the dead , great and small ;they stood before the throne, and books were opened, then another book was opened, which is[the Book] of life. And the dead were judged (sentenced) by what they had done [their whole way of feeling and acting, their aims and endeavors] in accordance with what was recorded in the books. So now, you can see how important it is not only to read the word, but also believe what you read. In the court of law you can only be judged by the laws written in the books of the laws of the land. How can you violate a law that is not written in the law book. It must be written before it can be a violation. I believe that one of the books that will be opened is the bible. It is one of the oldest book recorded unto this day.

I believe that our lives are going to be played back before us as if it were on a giant tv set. We won't be able to deny that it is us, because it will show the time and place. But thanks be to God that through Jesus Christ our Lord, our sins have been removed if we would believe His word and except Him as our personal savior right now and believe that He died for our sin, then you are saved. But remember when a baby is born that is just the beginning, it has to be cared for until it can learn to take care of it's self. Fine a bible believing church, for there is so much you need to learn. Matt.11:29 reads, take my yoke upon you and learn or Me, for I am gentle (meek) and humble (lowly) in heart, and you will find rest for your souls.

A New Walk and a New Talk

In the previous chapter I talked about new born babies, well I would like to continue that trend of thought if I may. As you know giving birth has a new process of it's own. Not only for the baby but for you also. I recommend that every first time mother take the time to take parenting classes. You'll be amazed how much you can learn from others. In the book of first peter 2:2reads. Like newborn babies you should crave the pure spiritual milk of the word, that by it you may be nurtured and grow unto (completed) salvation. Yes this is a learning process, but what isn't.? When we are born we know absolutely nothing. Some one had to take the time to teach us how to live. So is every one that is born again, somebody has to love us enough to teach us how to grow in grace and, in the knowledge of our Lord and savior Jesus Christ. The bible is a letter or history of the master plan that God used to show us how we could be reconciled back to our god given position. Not everyone will except the plan of salvation but that doesn't have to be you, the choice is yours.

Christmas

Can you believe that it is Christmas all ready, when I was a child it seemed as though Christmas would never get here. But now that time of the year seems to roll around so fast. In the bible it talk about when the days would be shorten and we would not to be able to tell summer from winter. I'm experiencing my seventy third Christmas I also have lived to see my third generation, and if Jesus tarries, in April of 2011, I would have lived to see my fourth. I can remember when the children were young , it would be one of the busiest times of the year. Having to shop for six children and a husband is not an easy thing to do, but, by Gods help we made it through. This year, I had dinner at my house at thanksgiving and Christmas, you are always glad when it is over.

A new year always represent's another chance to do the thing that you didn't get done in the previous year. And a chance to make a commitment to God if you have not already done so. We sing a song sometimes and it go's like this. Don't let it be said to late, to late, to enter the golden gate. Keep in mind the price that was paid that you and I could do so. It is going to take a lot of faith to get through this year, we may en counter something that we have never had before, but by faith we can do all things. Pastor Troy (my son) preached a sermon titled "Mustard Seed Faith." Taken from the book of Matt.17:20 ... if you have faith like a grain of mustard seed you can say to this mountain move from yonder place and it will move. I think that we are tested in our faith from time to time. First of all your request must line up with Gods will for your life. Your request can't be something that God has not planned for your future. He knows what plans He has for you. Jer. 29:11. For I know the thoughts I have for you, says the Lord, thoughts for your welfare and peace and not evil. To give you hope in your final outcome. Heb. 11:1 talks about now faith. The principles of faith is the substances of things hope for and the evidence of things not seen. We have the proof and it is found in the word of God, the Bible. Faith only come by hearing and the thing that you must be hearing is the word of God. Now, we that have children know sometimes we are shouting at them, and as the old folks would say, that it went in one ear and out the other, or there inter- ear didn't hear a thing you said. Or we have shouted at them so much until they have closed there inter-ear. Rom; 11:8 As it is written, God has given them a spirit of (an attitude) of stupor, eyes that should not see and ears that should not hear, [that has continued] down until this very day. So don't think you can get anything from God until you line up with His word, and His will for your life. Every year we make a resolution to do something this year that we didn't get done last year. Now let us take inventory of all them we have made over the years. Now check and see how many of them you kept. Well I don't remember keeping any of mine, so I just don't bother to make them any more. Every year we celebrate having made it though the old year and we pray in the new year. The way things are going for our country we are going to need a LOT of prayer for the in-coming year. I don't know about you, but my hope is built on nothing less then Jesus Christ and His righteousness. And this is the only hope for our nation. Earlier we were talking about faith that could move mountains, well the spirit of God knows the real thing when He sees it. Act 19:12 Reads. So that handkerchiefs which had touched his skin were carried away and put upon the sick, and their diseases left them and evil spirits came out of them. V. (13), Then some of the traveling Jewish exorcists (man who adjure evil spirits) also undertook to call the name or Jesus over those that had evil spirits, saying, I charge you by the name of Jesus whom Paul preaches! V.(15), but one evil spirit retorted, Jesus I know, and Paul I know, but who are you? V.(16). Then the man in whom spirits dwelt leaped upon them, mastering two of them ,and was violent against them that they dashed out of that house [in fear] stripped naked and wounded .

TO HELL AND BACK

I'm sure you heard about the thirty three man that were trapped in a mine for over two months. Well, the meaning of hell is being in a place of confinement. So we can say that those man have been to hell and back, and lived to tell it. I was so glad when they lifted the last man out. But there is a hell that will lead to a place where there will be no escape route out. As you follow the life and death of Christ you will find that He not only payed the penalty for our sins but, he also went down into the bowls of the earth and gave salvation to those who died before His appearance, yet embracing by faith His promise of redemption even long after there death. So after He had put on His spiritual body He paid hell a visit setting free those that had died in faith.

Also, He took the keys of death and hell from the devil so he could no longer hold captive those who died in the faith. 1cor.15:55 Reads. O death where is your victory. O death where is your sting. It is so refreshing to know that when we leave this life, we are going to a place of rest. We have safely entered into two thousand eleven even though we don't know what the future holds, but, this we do know if Jesus leads us we will make it home someday.(heaven) there is a saying we learned many years ago, and it goes like this. This life will soon be passed but, only what we do for Christ will last. We have many hopes and dreams for this, but don't forget the most important thing of all, if you should die today where would you spend eternity?. It is Gods master plan that you go to Heaven when you die.(Now heaven is wherever Jesus is.)

This generation seems to think that they can do what they always did and get a different outcome. But it doesn't work like that. Because if you do what you always did, you will get what you always got. But if you change your direction then you will end up in another place.

Our Threefold Nature

When God created man He gave him a three fold nature, a soul a body and spirit. Now if you line them up this is how they go, you have a body, in your body lives your spirit and your soul. Now your soul and spirit will live forever but your body must be changed into a eternal state. Wherever your spirit lives it will be forever. Now here is where you come in. While you live, you can make the decision where that will be. I know you are thinking, if I die and my body goes back to dust then where will this eternal body come from? Thanks for asking. Do you remember me saying that your spirit can't die? Well I told you because your spirit came from God It can't die so when you fall asleep (die) then your spirit goes back to the God that gave it to you in the first place. Then He puts it wherever He wishes it to go.

It reminds me of how a debit card works. When you take it to the bank and put it in the teller machine to do your transaction, when you are finished the card comes back to you, because it was yours in the first place. There is a scripture that says that the dead know nothing but the living know that they must die. But I believe when they wake up that it will be a new ball game. Only what you do while your alive will determine your destiny. It's very simple, right where you are acknowledge that you are a sinner (all of us were at one time in our lives) and repent of your sins, then ask the holy spirit to come into your heart, now by faith believe that He did. Now look for a bible believing church not just any church, but one that believes in the bible. Ask the Holy spirit to show you which one to go to, and He will.

The Just Shall Live By Faith

We have talked about how to make peace with God, now we will talk about how to keep that peace. It is very simple, the just shall live by faith. Now you must acquire an appetite for the word of God. In the book of Roms. 10:14 Says, But, how can they call on Him whom they have never heard of, or have faith in, and how can they hear without a preacher. Now a preacher is a special messenger from God. The five fold ministry is for the building up of the church. We that are born again must have a study diet of the word of God. When I was raising my children there was a saying put out by one of the milk companies that said, you will never out grow your need for milk. Well, I believe that you'll never out grow your need for the word of God. I have found that the more word that you have, the more faith you have. We are experiencing two Kingdoms, the Kingdom of darkness [this world] and the Kingdom of Gods dear Son. The first one is visible, the second one is invisible. When you are born again your spiritual eyes will become opened and you will be able to enter the spiritual world and then and only then, you will be able to understand the things of God. Sometimes at our church I will get feedback. They are saying that they don't understand what they hear. Well it is because their spiritual ears are not open. Do you remember me saying that when I got saved that I didn't remember a thing that the pastor said, that I went forward as the spirit lead me. I had begun to hunger and thirst for the true and living God. You must do the same thing, don't stop until you have Him, the one that your soul longs for.

I Have Come This Far By Faith

I received the Lord at the age of nineteen. That has been fifty four years ago, and by His grace sometimes I feel like that commercial about the energizer bunny, I just keep going and going. Once you get into the light of Gods love, it grows brighter and brighter. When you learn how to exercise your faith the Christian walk is very exciting. About two years ago I became very ill in the middle of the night. A lady came to the side of my bed. I remember thinking, what does that mean. I got up to go to the bathroom, and she came again. While I was in the bathroom I became very sick. My granddaughter was sleeping in my room that night. I became very weak, I remember asking the Lord to give me enough strength to make it back to my room, and He did. Then I told my granddaughter to call for help, and she did. I believe that the lady I saw was an angel, and she came to warn me. We were in Alabama when the hurricanes hit new Orleans, we were planning to come to Ohio for my mothers one hundredth birthday. I knew that my car was acting up, so I made plans to rent a car for that trip. On the day we were going to leave everybody were leaving Alabama in fear of the storm. When I called the place where I had made plans to rent a car, the man said, lady there isn't a car left on this lot to rent to you. So I took my car to the place that I had it serviced and he said that perhaps it would make it. So we headed for Ohio. Now

Ohio is about a thousand miles from Ala. I must say that the Lord did bless us, we were only about thirty miles from Toledo when the transmission went out on it. Thank God for AAA. They came and loaded the car on there truck and we were in Toledo in about forty five minutes. There are many stories that I could tell about how God has brought us through.

How We Got To Toledo, Ohio

I was born and raised in Michigan. We lived about forty five miles south of Detroit, MI. My dad work for the Ford motor Co. For forty five years. When he started there they were paying only fifty cents per hour. We had always lived in the country. My dad loved the country life style. We had pigs, cows, horses, chickens and goats, I'm sure that you get the picture. I had never lived in the city. Sometimes we would go to visit family that lived there. I just didn't like the city. It was just to fast for me. After we got married we moved to Milan, Mich. After about nine years my husband had moved on and I decided to remarry. One day I was listening to the radio and a church service from Trinity Faith came on from Toledo Ohio. The Lord said to me, I want you and your family to move to Toledo, Ohio. I didn't believe what I had just heard. But believe it or not that is just where I've been for over forty years. In Milan, MI, It was seven of us. We had a fire and the house we lived in burned to the ground. So one of the trustees of our church offered us a small three room house that they let the hired help live in. They lived on a forty acre estate and from time to time they needed help out there. It was much to small for our family but that was all we could find then. We made do. Later on he added three more rooms to it, and that made it a lot better. Well, his wife died. And after a while him and I started dating and we got married, and I told him about what the Lord had told me about Toledo, Ohio and we begin to look for a house here. When we first moved in, the children hated it here. They told me how when we first moved here that they would go up into the attic and cry and thank of ways that they could move back to the country. But after they were here for a while you couldn't pay them to go back there to live. That has been over forty years ago and all of them are still here. (my fifth child died here in two thousand six.)

How The Christ Garden Of Prayer Church Began

For many years I served in different churches. I was born again in a church in Milan, MI. When I was nineteen. We were there for nine years. Then we moved to Ohio in nineteen sixty six. We went back to the Milan church in sixty seven. Then in nineteen seventy five I joined a church that was in my back yard so to speak. I was there for six years. By then the children begin to have children of there own. I begin to notice that my grandchildren were unchurched. So I decided to start a church in my home for them, and any one that wanted to come. On Saturdays I would go to there homes and comb the girls hair and make sure that they had clean clothes to wear, and on Sunday morning I would pick them up for church. I received a promise from the Lord. My late husband died in nineteen eighty three. I closed the church and went to California for a while. After I returned to Ohio. I attended a church that needed a pastor. So when they ask me if I would take the job, after praying about it I excepted . By then my eldest son had been reclaimed and came too work with me in the ministry. One day I was at the church and the Lord spoke to me and said, Ethel, if you will walk with me in the beauty of holiness I will save your children unto the third and fourth generation. Thanks be to God if Jesus tarry in April I will see my fourth generation. My son Troy is our pastor and have been for the last seven years. I am now their Overseer.

Coping In The New Generation

These days remind me of the days of Noah. God trusted him with some plans that He had for the whole world. Gens.6:7. So the Lord said that I will destroy man kind whom I have created from off of the face of the earth. I hope that you take the time to read the accounts of our history and see for yourself just who is really in charge of this earth. I know last year so many awful things happened in this world. But, it is like Noah's day we have been put on notice that God is about to make His move on this wicked world. It is up to us to get ready and stay ready. We are living in a time when anything goes. Now a day you have to be careful of what you watch on TV, because it will vex your spirit. Remember that your eyes are the windows to your soul. You can't allow all of that corruption to enter your spirit, the bible says that God will not dwell in a unclean temple. Think about your house, we have our limits in our home, we may let things go for a while, but then out comes the mop and broom and the pine sol. I'm sure you get the picture. All of us have TV's in our homes but we must choose what we watch so we will not corrupt our spirit, there by causing the Holy spirit to move. I remember when they were not allow to say a curse word on TV. But now days anything goes, you can say and do almost anything. I usually retire for the night about ten pm. After watching the late news, I will watch some late night show until I fall asleep. But things got so bad that I just could not watch any more. You have to be careful of what you allow to enter your eye gate because it will corrupt your spirit. Believe it or not these are the last days before the second coming of the Lord. I believe it and so should you. We must set standards for our children or when they grow up they will have no example to draw from. So think about what you are leaving behind for your children, something's are priceless. The old saying, do as I say and not what you see me do, didn't work then and it won't work now. Remember our children can read us like a book. They are much more impressed by what they see then what they hear, specially if it is coming from a parent. The eye gate is much more powerful then the ear. This is why we that are parents have to tell our children over and over again. And this is why we have to hear the word of God over and over again. Someone said that we have thick skulls. We don't always get it the first time, we have to keep on hearing and hearing the word of God.

Everything is Changing

We expect things to change for the better, and something's are but something's are changing for the worse, and it is having a negative reaction on us all. Have you notice that the crime rate has gone up a hundred per cent lately. The bible talk about the increase in lawlessness in the last days. Well just look around you. It isn't safe any more night or day. I can remember when you didn't have to lock your doors, if you were just going to the store and coming right back. Now days you had better lock yourself in and don't open them for anyone unless you are sure that it is safe. The evil forces are being loosed on this world, because we have forgotten God. But it isn't to late, God has a MASTER PLAN for all who will except it. all you have to do is repent and ask Jesus to come into your heart right now, and believe that He did. Then start your new walk with Him, and always remember He is always right there by your side. At our church I am doing a series on the book of Revelation

It's not an easy book to understand, but the bible say's that if you just read it you will receive a blessing, I don't know about you, but I need all the blessings that I can get. Anyway I will be doing part two on it. The historians believe that some part of Revelations has already been fulfilled, I agree with that. But I believe that the greater part of it has not. We are studying about the seven church that were in Asia. We must understand that Gods plans are forever settled in the Heavens. One of the things that He told John the revelator was that, He is Alpha and Omega the beginning and the ending, so you see, He already has His plan in order from the very beginning. It is like the people that made the road map, when you get it is already finished. Don't you think the power that made you has more knowledge then we do? Don't you know that the man that build the house is greater then the house he build?. Just because you can't see Him with your natural eyes does not reduce His ability. This is a faith walk. Remember that God is a spirit, and those that worship Him must do so in spirit and in truth. And that truth is in the word of God. We that practice the word of God know that no matter how bad things look , that through the blood of Jesus we have everything that the Bible says that we will have, first of all, the most important thing is that we need to make peace with God. That could only be done through the shed blood of Jesus. Once that is done then we know, if we trust Him then and only then all things are possible. Through the blood of Jesus we have excess to the kingdom of God while we live. Yes, every now and then our faith is tested, and we pass the test then and only then we receive a promotion, you in God we move from faith to faith. But I have learned that you will always keep moving in this faith walk until you hear Him say well done my good and faithful servant. We may not know it but, we all have faith in something. It may be our jobs, or some other thing that we don't realize that we are trusting in. Have you thought about this. When we get a job, we don't get paid that same day, we are told that we have to work for two weeks before we receive our first pay check. Well that means that you have to believe by faith in what you are told and work for two weeks before being paid. That's faith. We have not seen God but we are convinced that He is who He says He is, and by faith we will receive all that He has promised us.

All Old Things Shall Pass Away

When we moved to Toledo, Ohio in nineteen sixty six, there were many older buildings here in the old west end where we live. In two thousand four I moved to the State of Alabama and I was there for five years. When I moved back to Ohio in two thousand nine, I noticed that many of the older buildings were being torn down, and new ones were being build. There was a school that I could see from my house. My children attended their before going to high school. It was called Robinson Jr high. Well, when I returned here almost three years ago they had build a new Jr. High school. But the old one was still standing, empty. Someone, in the beginning of this year begin to tear it down. The building was ninety years old. This is happening all over the city. It just goes to show that all old things shall pass a way, and all things shall become new.

This is one of the things that I loved about being born again. When the holy spirit came into my heart, I felt like I was brand new all over. I received a new attitude, the old song said, my hands look new and my feet did too. Well my hands looked the same but I felt renewed on the inside. Believe me my life was headed in a new direction. It is like getting married, you really have to experience it to understand how it feels. When you really mean what you are saying, then and only then will you find out what it is like. When you and your mate took those vows, nothing changed but by law you were no longer single. Well, the same thing happened when you are born again figuratively you are the same but spiritually you have changed. In marriage the two of you have become one. When you are born again you are no longer the same you have taken on a new life in Christ Jesus by faith. Now it is time to grow in faith and in the knowledge of our Lord and savior Jesus Christ. The true change starts in the mind. ref. 2cor.4:16. Do not be discouraged, our outer man, self is decaying, our inter self is being renewed day by day. You must be able to see the change in yourself, you will feel a drawing toward the things of God. You will want to hear the things that leads to life and happiness. You will find yourself submitting to the will of God and enjoying every minute of it.

Having a Good Foundation

Everything that is build must have a good foundation. We that are in the faith of our Lord and savior Jesus Christ, must build our faith on a solid foundation. There is no other foundation that is more sure then the word of God. In the book Luke,6:48 &49 talks about how we that are in the faith must build. And what our ladder end will be if we don't. I talked about the school in my back yard, Robinson jr high. Well I was taking my dog for a walk and when I looked over at it, it was one big pile of rocks. It just goes to show that nothing on this earth will last forever. I am reminded of something Jesus said in the bible. Matt. 24:2. Says. That as great a building as the temple was, although it took forty years to build it. But it would come a time when one stone would not be left upon another. As you know that came to pass many years ago.

This is why we teach so strongly about this system, someday it will be replaced with a new and better one, one that can not be defiled by any other system.

What Does The Bible Say About This System

From the beginning this was a great place to be. And someday it will be again. All that it needs is a system that can't be lead by an ungodly way of thinking. Who knows a product better then it's maker. No one. The earth was made by God and He Knows best how to run it. We might as well let Him guide us because He is going to do so anyway in the end. Gens. 1:1. Says, In the beginning God created the heavens and the earth.

When man was put on this earth he was in the state of innocence. They had been given a nature that came from God, he knew no sin. So for a while he lived in that state of mind, sinless, or innocent. At that time the world was in perfect harmony, can you believe it, that there was no sin in this world. Before sin can take root it must be planted. Now the only place that it can be planted is in the mind. Corruption is a mind thing. The bible says as a man thinks, in his mind so is he. So, if we can control the way we think, then we can do the right thing in the sight of God. Oh yes it can be done.(phil. 2:5.) Reads, let this mind be in you that was also in Christ Jesus----. So you see it is very important to have the same mind that Christ Jesus had while He was on earth, and did the things that He did, and He is the only man that God said is sinless. So it must start in the mind. Now it can only happen through faith. Now the only way that you can receive faith is by hearing, but the thing that you must be hearing is the word of God. I am sure that you are seeing on the news, the things that are going on in the middle east. Well, when Jesus was here, in body. He told the disciple about the days we are living in today. Yes, these are the signs of His second coming. A great price was paid that you would not be destroyed. Jesus is the only way for that to happen. Revolution after revolution is taking place in the world. We are on shak'y ground all over this world. Jesus said, when you see these things, to look up for our redemption is near. We are going to write about the book of Revelation in the next part of this book, very soon. If we would only believe the gospel that has been recorded in the word of God, the bible, we would see many things that are hidden from the rest of the world.

The Book of Revelation

This is the only book in the Bible that promises the reader that they would receive a blessing for just reading it. This book is about consummation. In it, the divine program of redemption is brought to fruition. This book focuses on prophetic events.

This book was written by John the revelator, as he is sometimes called. He was exiled on the island of Patmos, some say in the hope that he would be eaten by some wild animal. But

God had other plans for him. While he was there, he saw Christ the King of Kings and the Lord of Lords in a vision, and was told things that no other human being had ever been told. John told about being in the spirit on the Lords day, and I heard a loud voice, behind me as of a trumpet, saying, I am the alpha and the omega, the first and the last, what you see write in a book and send it to the seven churches which are in Asia: . . .Then I turned to see the voice that spoke to me. I saw seven golden lamp stands, and in the mist of the seven stands, one like the Son of Man, clothed with a garment down to His feet and girded about the chest with a golden band.. . .and when I saw Him I fell at His feet as dead. But He laid His right hand on me, saying to me, do not be afraid; I am the first and the last. In chapter two He gives John instruction concerning the seven churches which were in Asia. The churches that were still there, even through they were ran by man, they were being govern by God. Let us look at the first church that He addressed. It was in the city of Ephesus. Then He directed His message to the angel of the church, He was referring to the pastor of the church. Make sure to honor your spiritual leaders if they are leading you in the right direction. Apostle Paul said, we should follow him as he followed Christ. But if he stop following Christ then we should stop following him. Every believer must make sure that they are being lead in the right direction. Their are many false leaders in the world these days. When you make your commitment to Christ make sure you are being lead in the right direction. Let's get back to the book of Revelations. Now to the church at Ephesus He praises them for the work they had done. But the one thing He had against them, is that they had left their first love. Matt.24:12. Talks about the love of the great body of people will grow cold because of the multiplied lawlessness and iniquity. Whatever there problems were it was going to cause Him to no longer be in there mist. The bible calls it, having a form of godliness, but denying the power there of. The Bible is the only road map that will lead you to the kingdom of God. To the church in Smyrna. I took note that they said they were poor, but the Lord said they were rich. Anybody that take God at His word and do it, you may not know it, but you are rich. The righteous is promised Gods favor in this life and in the life to come. I notice that

He put a time limit on there suffering and even if it cost them their lives, they had much more to look forward to in the life to come. Everybody knows that this life will soon be passed, but only what we do for Christ will last. The third church He talked about was the church at Pergamum. They were dealing with satanic spirits but still trying to hold on to there convictions. Now that just won't work. You can't service two masters, you will love one and hate the other. He also commanded them to repent, or He would fight against them with the sword of His mouth. He also promised those who over came, He would give them a new name that no one would know or understand, but he to whom it was given. The fourth church that He addresses is the church at Thayatira. He first started by praising them for their love, faith, service, and patient endurance. Then He went on to say, that there recent works were more numerous then their first ones. Then He told them about their faults. And what He was going to do about them, if they didn't repent.

The fifth church was in the city of Sardis. This was His message to them. You are supposed to be alive, but in reality you are dead. Then He gave them a chance to do better, by arousing themselves and keeping awake and giving strength to that which remain and vigor to that which is about to die. He went on to say that all of their works was unexceptionable in the sight of God. How would you like to get to heaven an find that report penned to your record. We that are leaders please read about the out come of these churches. And make sure that you are not guilty of these thing or something worse. It is a terrible thing to fall into the hands of a angry God. The sixth church that He had John to address was the church in the city of Philadelphia. He open by saying that these are the words of the Holy one and the true one. He who has the keys of David, and if He open a door no one could shut it. Who shut and no one could open it. He said to them I know that you only have a little power, but yet you have kept my word and guarded my message and have not renounced my name. I will also keep you from the hour of testing that will come upon all the world. The seventh and last church that He spoke about was the church in the city of Laodicea. He said to them that He knew their works, and they were neither hot or cold, I would that you were hot or cold. He told them because your neither hot or cold, I will spit you out of my month, because you are lukewarm. This church needed to make up their mind if they were going to serve God or not. I class these people as church jumpers, don't know what that want or where they want to be, they refuse to stick to anything. We have had some of those kind in our church, and if you are a pastor, I know that you have also. They are saying that they are rich and have need of nothing. Now they don't know it but they are wretched, miserable, poor, blind, and naked. How short sighted can you get and understand that your not in the faith. He told John to tell them to purchase from Me gold refined and tested by fire, that they may be truly wealthy, and in need of nothing.

Christ the Lamb

We sometimes down play the roll that Jesus had and will have in the kingdom of God and the kingdom of this world. The kingdom of this world is known as the kingdom of darkness. We are being told from the word of God that all things will be returned back to the God that giveth in the first place. Yes, it is a process but it will happen. Here in the book of revelation, we are able to take a look at the rule and reign of Christ the king. Chapter five of revelation, it talked about the scroll that none was worthy to open it. And John began to cry because no one was worthy enough to open it. Then one of the Elders of the Sanhedrin, . . . See the Lion of the tribe of Judah ,the root of David, He can open the scroll and break the seven seals. Now, when the seals were opened it talked about the things that would happen on earth. One of the things that happen was He was empowered to take the peace out of the earth, so that men slaughtered one another. Also one of the things that was going to happen after it's seal was opened, the stars fell from the sky, and the sky rolled up like a scroll and vanished. We sing a song in church, and it goes like this, build your hopes on things that are for eternity and hold to Gods unchanging hand. Another judgment is when a great mountain was thrown into the sea, and the mountain was on fire. And a third of the sea turned into blood. And a third of the living creatures in the sea died. And a third of the ships were destroyed. . . . and a huge star fell from heaven , burning like a torch,

Dropping on the rivers and on the springs of waters . . . and the name of the star is wormwood, and a third part of the water was changed into wormwood, and many people died from using the water, because it was very bitter. (rev.9:3.) Then out of the smoke came locusts, on the earth. And the power of a scorpion was given to them. They were told only to attack such humans that do not have the seal of God on the foreheads. They were not permitted to kill them, but to torment them for five months; and the pain was like that of a sting of a scorpion. And those days people will seek death, but they will not be able to die. The locusts resembled horses equipped for battle. And the rest of them, people, who were not killed, did not repent of their murders, or there practice of sorceries or there sexual vices or their thefts. I would like to go back and talk about the two seals. In chapter seven it talks about the seals that came from God. Verse four tells how many were sealed and who they were. One hundred and forty four thousand, and they were all from the tribe of Israel. Chapter fourteen, verse nine, talks about another stamp or mark that was given to those who paid homage to the beast. This mark was put on there forehead or there hand. Those persons shall have to drink of the wine of God's wrath and indignation. Chapter 19:13. Gives a vision of Christ in His glorified state. He is dressed in a robe dyed by being dipping in blood, and the title by which He is called is The word of God. Chapter 20:2. Tells about an angel from heaven was given the power to bind satan and cast him into the bottomless pit for a thousand years. After that he must be loosed for a short time. (Verse 4) Then I saw thrones , and sitting on them were those who were giving authority to act as judges and to pass sentence was given to them. Now those that are sitting on the judgment seat are those that took part in the first resurrection.[ref.] I Thess. 4:16-17 .The Lord Himself will come down from heaven with a loud cry of summons, and the cry of an archangel and with the blast of the trumpet of God. And those who died in Christ, shall rise first. V. (17). Then we that are alive on earth, shall rise with them, in the clouds to meet the Lord in the air. Then we will always be with the Lord through eternities. Rev. Chapter 21:1. Then I (John) saw a new heaven and a new earth, for the former earth had vanished , and their were no more sea.(V 2.) And I saw the holy city, the new Jerusalem coming down from

Heaven from God, arrayed like a bride adorned for her husband; then I heard a mighty voice from the throne and I heard it say, See ! The abode of God is with men, He will live among them; and they shall be His people, and God shall personally be with them and be their God. (V 4.) God shall wipe away every tear from their eyes; and death shall be no more, neither shall their be anguish or grief or pain, for all old things have passed away. (v,7) He who is victorious shall inherit all things, and I will be God to him and he shall be My son. (V) 8. But as for the cowards and ignoble and the contemptible and the cravenly liking in courage and the cowardly submissive and as for the unbelieving and faithless, and as for the depraved and defiled with abomination , and as for murderers and the lewd and adulterous and the practiced or magic arts and the idolaters and all liars shall have their part in the lake that burns with fire and brimstone. This is the second death.

Note: As you read this book, Gods master plan for humanity, that it will inspire you to catch a hold to the faith of our Lord and savior Jesus the Christ, and be blessed and highly favored by Him. Amen.

I dedicate this book to every bible believing God fearing person that have a passion for lost souls everywhere in this world. To the one who might not pick up a bible and read the word of God. But in joy reading this version of the word of God that has been broken down into layman's terms. When you have finished reading it please pass it on to someone that might get an insight into the word of God. And decide to put the word of God into action in there lives. The word has the power to transform a person's life if by chance they would get a hold of faith. I am sure that we all are seeing what is happening all over the world. Earthquakes, tsunamis, radiation leaking into there water and there food supply. These are some of the signs of His soon return. I have written about the end times spoken about in the book of Revelation. Know this that He is coming as the thief dose in the night, when you are asleep. Please don't let Him find you with your work undone.

Can you believe that we have experienced another life changing storm in the south. I talked about my years in the south earlier in this book. We were there when the hurricane hit new Orleans. Alabama is about a hundred miles from there. I was watching the news last week, and the mayor was talking about how about forty per cent of the city is still in disrepair. There's many homes still standing unattended to. That makes the landscape look bad. All though they are better off in someways, but there is much work to be done. Just think about having gone through that storm, and every time the wind picks up, having to remember what that storm was like.

We moved to Toledo, Ohio. In the sixty's . We had been here about a year. A real bad tornado came through our city. When I was a child I can remember hiding under the bed when it stormed. The thunder and lighting was so frightening. I found myself praying that it would pass. The year the tornado came through Toledo, it was a bad one. Tree's were down, and we lost our power for about a week. There was a large tree between our house and our neighbors, fell. The food in the refrigerator spoiled. We were from the county, and used to hard times anyway. Now when the hurricane hit new Orleans, we in Alabama felt the affect from the strong wind's . The light's were out for about a week, also. A family that attended the same church we were, had a generator, and invited us over for dinner. We were very thankful. We were tire of eating cold cuts. But we finally got our power back. Like the old saying goes, you never miss your water until your well runs dry.

I wrote about the beginning of creation in a earlier chapter or this book. I talked about the earth and it's new beginning also. One of the things that make God, God, is His way's are not like our way's. Nor His through's like our through's. Remember everything God does, He does it with eternity in mind. On the other hand, we do just the opposite, we, most of the time seam to think short term. We look for quick gratification. It bring to mine a story I heard about a person that was called to the ministry by God. And they told God that thy would preach the gospel. After much pray and preparation, they excepted the call. He decided to pastor. So he started a small church.

When the church begin to grow, they appointed a deacon board. Then the church building was getting to small, so they went to the deacon board and told them that they were going to build a bigger church. But the deacons told them that if they went ahead with there plans, that they would look for another pastor. But the pastor had some news for them. They said, you did not hire me and you cant fire me. That's the way it is when we think we can tell God what to do.

Let us get back to the times and seasons that we are living in today. It is not just the weather that is doing it's own thing. It is everything and everybody. When I was growing up in the thirties & forties, government stood for something. Now days everybody think that they can run the country better then our leaders. This is what I call the know it all generation. Remember we had over two years to decide who we believed would be best suited for the job. Now that you have put them in office, stand by your chose. Pray that God will be there guide. For only (God) knows what the future holds. That's like deciding to have a baby, and when the baby arrive, then you change your mine. Well as you know, that just wont work. We use to say, when the going get tough, then the tough get going.

This week I saw on the news that Osama Ben Laden had been killed. And our president and his staff was the master minds be hide this victory. I'm waiting to see how long his approval rating will continue to go up. Longer then the last one did, I hope. It takes a mature person to have a study mind, and pray for our country and it's leaders. Well, spring has arrived. We have two cottonwood trees in our front yard. They are beautiful this time of the year. I can tell by the trees, when they start to bloom that spring has arrived. I have to look for something good to smile about at the beginning of each day. I don't always find it, but I'm going to keep looking. I have found that if I start my day with pray, that the day seems to go better. I was watching Joel Olsteen, and he was talking about the power of laughter.

A merry heart is good like medicine and a cheerful mind works healing, but a broken spirit dries up the bones.

Proverbs. 17:22

I must admit that there are not many things going on around us these days that make us laugh. But you must create the atmosphere that will lead you into a joyful spirit. In nineteen fifty three, I married into the Thomas family. I was very young at that time. We believed that if you were going to live with another person that you must be man and wife. I heard a pastor say, no wed, no bed. And that's what we believed. In my generation, shacking up with a person that you were not married to was almost unheard of. I'm not saying that you should marry the first person that come along. But what I am saying is wait until you are sure that is the person that you are willing to spend the rest of your life with. Do re-search into the back ground of that person. Don't believe everything they tell you. If it looks to good to be true, it probably is not true. There are two things that you must consider, can this person be trusted. And because marriage is made in heaven, is this union ordained by God. Young people and older people alike please keep your mind and body under subjection. You will save yourself a lot of heart ack, and trouble. I am speaking from experience. Some say that experience is the best teacher. But I believe that if you see a detour sign, that you best pay attention to the sign. You have to much to lose if you pick the wrong mate. And if there are children in the mix, then you are really in a jam. Also, if you decide to shack up with someone, there is a legal side to consider. Common law marriage very from state to state. Believe me when I tell you that Gods way is the best way. It bring to mine about a couple who were in there latter years. They decided to get marred, all I know for sure is that they did, and the marriage lasted about six months. That could have been any of us. Believe me I know how that feels. Thank God for His people who can pick up the pieces and go on with the rest of there life. But getting back to young people, you have your whole life ahead of you, take your time and be sure you are compatible with the choice you make.

There is a small town in Alabama that was hit, I can't remember the name of it, but I remember the church taking food for those who were forced to live in shelters. At my house in Ala. We experienced very high winds, closes to a hundred miles per hour. My dad had a shelter in the back yard, with a tin roof and a cement floor. In the summer time, he and my step mother would almost live out there. They had a stove for cooking out there and a table, chairs, a TV. They ran a phone line out there also. There was a large oak tree out there also. The wind blow some of the limes down, they fell on that roof and knocked part of it down. It also hit the roof of the house just clipping a small part of it. We were blessed, that was all the damage we suffered. Thank God for home insurance. I've been back in Ohio for three years. For the last two years we have been getting tornado warnings, but they all seem to go around us. In Erie county, last year, they lost there police station, there high school, school buses, homes, cars. The list goes on and on. They were bless only seven people lost their lives. It looked like a war zone after the storm passed. I know you must be thanking, where is God in all of this. Thanks for asking. He is where He is and where He always will be. Being the great God that He is, and always will be. In this book I wrote about the book of Revelation. It tells about how things will be when Christ the King comes back to repossess the Kingdom of this world. It was made by him, and He is coming back to take back that which was His in the first place. After watching the devil and his demons destroy this once beautiful earth that He created it to be. He will re- establish His Kingdom, putting to death all who walk after the flesh. We've had two thousand years to repent, and except Jesus as our Lard and savior, but look it is not to late. While you read these words, just bow your head and ask Jesus to come into your heart right now. See how easy that was. Now if you believe that Jesus died for your sins, by faith, you are saved. Now ask the Lord to show you where you must go to feed your faith. Make sure that it is a bible believing church so you can grow in grace and in the knowledge of our lord and savior Jesus the Christ.

And God saw everything that He had made, and behold,
it was good and very good, and He approved it completely.
And the evening and the morning was the sixth day.

Gens. 1;31. (The Amplified Bible)

The End Of Man's Government Is At Hand

The old folk used to tell there disobedient children that, don't you know that I brought you into this world, and I will take you out! Well when it comes to our creator and maker, when He decides to end this system, He really mean what He said. You that study your bible, will bring to mind the story in the bible about Noah and the ark.

Then the Lord said, My spirit will not always dwell and strive with man, for he also is flesh; but his days shall be 120 years.

Genesis 6;3.

History has repeated it's self time and time again. The pastor used to say, that it was water that time, but it will be fire next time.

But the day of the Lord will come like a thief, and then the heavens will vanish (pass a way)with a thunderous crash, and the (material) elements [of the universe] will be dissolved with fire, and the earth and the works that are upon it will be burned up.

2 Peter 3;10.

Our God is not a man, that He should lie. When I read that verse in the bible, I said to my self. Who would He lie to. Most people that lie (or deceive someone else) is because they have fear of the other person finding out the truth. Will someone please tell me, who is powerful enough to intimidate God. Everything we have came from Him. And by the way, the things that we have is just a loan. We brought nothing into this world, and believe me, we will take nothing out.

That brought to mind a story the minister told a my dads funeral. He said that there was a very rich man, the Dr. Told him that he should put his house in order, for he was going to die. Now he cooked up a plan, so he could take it all with him. He call his three closes friends to his bed side and told them just what he wanted done when he died. This was the plan. He took all of his money and divided it into three parts. And this is what he told them to do. Just before the undertaker closed the casket, they were to rush up and put the money inside, just before the lid was closed. After the funeral was over, his three closes friends ask one another if they had carried out there friends wishes. The first one confessed that he had some pressing bills to pay. So he took the money and paid his bills. The second one confessed that he had a sick child, and he spent the money on his sick child. The third friend begin to fuss at the others, then he said, I wrote him a check.

Let us get back to the book of Revelations. There has been a misunderstanding about the one hundred and forty four thousand that is talked about in chapter seven. Those that were sealed were the jews that were given a second chance to be saved. The jews were Gods chosen people. God chose them because they were a very small tribe of people. And God said that He would use them for His glory. Now you that are bible scholars know that God blinded the jews as to drift in the Gentiles. Now in Gods eyes, there are only two classes of people. Jew and Gentile. After the Gentile dispensation is completed, He promised that the jews would have a second chance to be saved. Now that is where those one hundred and forty four thousand comes in, they are what we call the remnant. Remnant, is what is lift at the end. Where some people got that they, (the remnant) were the only ones that would make it to heaven, I have no idea.

After this I looked and a vast host appeared which no one could count, gathered out of every nation .from all tribes and people and languages. These stood before the throne and before the Lamb: they were attired in white robes, with palm branches in their hands.

Revelation; 7;9.

According to the word of God, the throne of God is in heaven. So if only the one hundred and forty four thousand are going there, then what are these(a number that no man can number) doing there.

Please study the bible for yourself. Find a bible believing church, that is teaching the unadulterated word of God. The bible is the only road map to heaven. There are no short cuts that will get you there any quicker. Have you ever been traveling and missed your turn. And when you found yourself you were miles out of the way. Then you had to go all the way back to where you got off the right road, in order to get back on the right road. The bible is the only road map that will put you on the road to heaven, and guarantee that you will make it there [heaven].

Let us look at the ninth chapter of the book of Revelation. I pray that you take these words to heart. Then believe the gospel that is written in this book [the bible] Here in the city of Toledo, Ohio. When there is a storm heading our way, we will hear a siren go off. This is to warn us that there is a threat or possibility that we are in danger. The bible was put here for that same reason, to warn us of what is going to happen to us if we don't do something about our sins.

And just as it was appointed for [all] men to die, and after that the judgment even so it is that Christ, having been offered to take upon Himself and bear as a burden the sins of many once and once and for all, will appear a second time, not to carry the burden of sin nor to deal with sin, but to bring to full salvation those who are [eagerly , constantly, and patiently] waiting for and expecting Him.

Hebrews 9;27;28 (AMPBV)

We have had plenty of time to receive the Lord as our personal savior. All you have to be concerned about is are you ready. If the Lord were to come for you in the next five minutes, would you be ready to go back with Him, I pray so. Time is running out. No man knows the time or the hour that His second coming will be. But we can be ready when He does come.

Then the fifth angel blew his trumpet, and I saw a star that had fallen from the sky to the earth; and to angels were given the key of the shaft of the Abyss (the bottomless pit). He opened the long shaft of the Abyss (the bottomless pit). And smoke like from a huge furnace puffed out of the long shaft, so that the sun and the atmosphere were darkened by the smoke from the long shaft. Then out of the smoke locusts came forth on the earth, and such power was granted them as the power the earth's scorpions have. They were told not to injure the herbage of the earth nor the green things nor any tree, but only (to attack) such human beings as do not have the seal (mark) of God on there foreheads. They were not permitted to kill them, but to torment (distress, vex) them for five months; and the pain caused them was like the torture of a scorpion when it stings a person. And in those days people will seek death and will not find it; and they will yearn to die, but death evades and flees from them.

Revelation 9; 1-6.

I pray that you who read this book, will not take it lightly. As sure as there is a God in the sky, these thing will surely come to pass. Now let us take a look at the spirit of the great harlot.

One of the seven angels who had the seven bowls then came and spoke to me ,saying , Come with me! I will show you the doom (sentence judgment) of the great harlot(idolatress) who is seated on many waters , (She) with whom the rulers of this earth has joined in prostitution (idolatry) and the wine of whose immorality the inhabitant of the earth have became intoxicated. And (the angel) bore me away (rapt) in the spirit into a desert, and I saw a woman seated on a scarlet beast that was all covered with blasphemous titles and he had seven heads and ten horns. The woman was robed in purple and scarlet and bedecked with gold, precious stones , and pearls, (and she was)holding in her hand a golden cup full of the accursed offenses and the filth of her lewdness and vice.

Revelation 17; 1-4

Note: As I said earlier, that these visions that John were having was while he (John) was in the spirit, on the Lords day. There are two kingdoms in operation in this world. The kingdom of darkness, and the kingdom of Gods dear Son. Now which kingdom is at work in your life? Whether you know it or not, one of these kingdoms is at work in your life. In th book of Galatians. 5;19. Now the works of the flesh are clear, they are immorality, impurity , indecency, Idolatry, sorcery, enmity, strife, jealousy, anger, selfishness, division, party spirit (factions, sects with peculiar opinions, heresies).Envy, drunkenness, carousing, and the like. I warn you beforehand, just as I did previously, that those who do such things shall not inherit the kingdom of God. Now in verse 22, tell how the kingdom of God operates. Whether you believe it or not, you are participating in one of these kingdom. One leads to life eternal, and the other leads to eternal damnation. Time is running out, please don't put it off, tomorrow is not promised to us, Jesus said, the day you hear my voice, do not harden your heart. If you are reading this book, please see it as the Lord speaking to you. No time is better then the present. Bow your head right where you are, now ask the Lord to come into your heart right now. Now if you did that and you believe with all your heart that He did, then you are born again. Now ask the Lord to lead you to a good church where you can grow in grace and the knowledge of our Lord and savior Jesus Christ. Let us get back to the book of Revelation. When we are born we have the ability, when we are old enough to make our own choices, then we can decide what kind of person that we want to be. Yes we are born with a sinful nature, but somewhere in life God will begin to deal with your soul. Early on in this book I talked about how that the Lord found me. I was not raised in a Christine home, it was just the opposite. But when I was twenty years old, I found my self looking for the one that my soul loved. As the old song goes, my soul just could not be contented, until I found the Lord. The bible says that, time and chance happen to us all. So when your time comes, take it. Now John the Revelator, when he got couch up in the spirit, he was seeing spiritual beings. Let us talk about how these being came into power. Do you remember when Adam and Eve were in the garden of Eden? Well guest who showed up there also! Yes you guest it, the serpent. Now the serpent had allowed the devil to inter into his spirit, and take it over. See, what the devil don't want you to know is if you don't let him in, then he will have no place to go. When God made man, He gave him the power of chose. After all He didn't make a robot, He made man in His own image and His likeness. He had a will and the ability to choose. So we know that both good and evil exist in the reformation of the earth. Yes we know how it got here. When Satan was cast out of heaven, he fell down to the earth. I believe that is why the earth was dark and empty, because Satan had made a mess of everything here. So when God decided to give the earth a new beginning, Satan became the prince of the air, with no place to go.

And if Adam and Eve had been obedient, them sin would have never entered into the flesh. So there disobedience caused the hold human family to enter into the sins of our forefathers.

Oh but look, here comes Jesus, and He's treading the wine press along. That spotless lamb of God.

As the song goes: behold the lamb of God, the precious lamb of God , I'll never know why He loved me so, that precious lamb of God.

I am ready to show you what will happen to the saints of the most high God, which is known as the bride of Christ, as she is called.

Let us rejoice and shout for joy, celebrate and ascribe to Him glory and honor, for the marriage of the lamb (at last) has come. And his bride has prepared herself. She has been permitted to dress in fine linen, dazzling in white-for the fine linen, represents the righteousness (the upright, the just, and godly living , deeds, and conduct, and right standing with God) of all the saints (God's holy people). Then(the angel said to me, write this down: Blessed (happy ,to be envied, called) are those who are summoned to the marriage supper of the Lamb. And he said to me (further) These are the true words (the genuine and exact declaration) of God.----After that I heard what sounded like the shout of a vast throng, like the boom of many pounding waves, and like the roar of terrific and mighty peals of thunder, exclaiming, Hallelujah (praise the Lord) for now the Lord our God the Omnipotent (the All-Ruler) reigns!

Revelations 19: 7 & 6

Continuing With The Bride of Christ

After that I saw the heavens opened, and behold a white horse [appeared]. The one who is riding it is called faithful and true. And he passed judgment and wages war in righteousness. His eyes, blazed like a flame of fire, and on His head are many kingly crowns and he had a title that He alone knew. He wore a robe dyed by dipping it in blood, and the title which He was called is the word of God. And the troops of heaven clothed in fine linen, dazzling and clean, followed Him on white horses. From his mouth goes forth a sharp sward with which He can smite the nations; and He will shepherd and control them with a staff or iron. He will tread the winepress of the wrath and indignation of God and All Ruler. And on His robe and on His thigh He has a name in scribed, King of Kings and Lord of Lords.

Revelation 19: 11-16.

I trust you have enjoyed reading the messages that are written in this book. May God bless you all.

Note: While ministering at church on Sunday, I was teaching on the fall of man. My mind went back to the creation of the earth, the six days it took to complete the re-construction of the earth, and what brought about the fall. But while constructing my sermon, it hit me. Now we know that God is a good God, and there is no evil in Him at all. So where did this evil spirit come from? So I went back to the fall. (Isaiah 14: 12-16) Remember, this is a double vision that Isaiah is having. First of all he is seeing the fall of Satan, and the destruction that he has caused to happen on the earth. But he also sees the punishment that he receives for doing so. He also sees his end. When he is put in a pit all a long. I hope you know that hell was not made for us, Gods creation. It was intended only for Satan and his followers. But because so many of us are bring lead by the flesh, hell has had to enlarge it's self. Please think about what you are doing to your self, and turn from your wicket ways by accepting Jesus as your lord and savior.